Acupressure for Tics Made Easy

An Illustrated Self Treatment Guide

Dr. Krishna N. Sharma

Disclaimer:

Information provided this book is meant to complement and not replace any advice or information from a health professional. The reader is encouraged to use good judgment when applying the information contained and to seek advice from a qualified professional if, and as, needed. The author reserves the right not to be responsible for the topicality, correctness, completeness or quality of the information provided. Liability claims regarding damage caused by the use of any information provided, including any kind of information which is incomplete or incorrect, will therefore be rejected.

Copyright Notice:

Published by the Amazon Group, USA

ISBN: 148194360X
ISBN-13: 978-1481943604

DEDICATION

To my Parents
Dr. L. Sharma
Smt. Chintamani Sharma

CONTENTS

ACKNOWLEDGMENTS

I wish to express my sincere gratitude to my beloved parents and family for their support, strength, love, help and for everything.

I would like to thank all my patients who put faith on me and blessed me the opportunity to treat them.

Last but not least I wish to avail myself of this opportunity, express a sense of gratitude and love to my friends for their love, encouragement and critical reviews.

PREFACE

It is my immense pleasure to present my twentieth book on Acupressure. This small book is a very small effort to help the patients with tics cop up with this problem. I wanted to write a book which may help the patients, their families and health professionals etc treat the patients. Since I have tried to keep the medical terms away as much as possible and there are lots and lots of illustrations, I hope you'll find it easy to administer.

I hope that this book will help convey to the readers some of the fascination that this subject matter holds for me.

Mumbai, India

Dr. Krishna N. Sharma
Email: dr.krisharma@gmail.com
Web: http://www.krishna.info.ms

DR. KRISHNA N. SHARMA

1 WHAT IS TIC

Tic is a sudden, repetitive, nonrhythmic motor movement or vocalization involving discrete muscle groups.

Classification:

The tics are classified in two ways:

- Motor or phonic Tics
- Simple or complex Tics
  - o Simple Motor Tics
  - o Simple Phonic Tics
  - o Complex Motor Tics
  - o Complex Phonic Tics

Motor Tics: These are movement-based tics affecting discrete muscle groups.

Phonic Tics: These are involuntary sounds produced by the nose, mouth, or throat.

Simple Motor Tics: These motor tics usually involve only one group of muscles, e.g. head jerking, eye blinking, or shoulder shrugging etc.

Simple Phonic Tic: These are common vocal tics e.g. sniffing, throat clearing, or grunting etc.

Complex Motor Tics: These are more purposeful-appearing and of a longer nature. It involves a cluster of movements and appear coordinated e.g. touching objects, touching people, or pulling at clothes.

Complex Phonic Tics: It includes echolalia (repeating words just spoken by someone else), palilalia (repeating one's own previously spoken words), lexilalia (repeating words after reading them).

2 WHAT IS ACUPRESSURE

Acupressure is an ancient Chinese alternative medicine technique. It is derived from acupuncture. It is based on the Traditional Chinese medicine's (TCM) acupuncture theory developed 5,000 years ago. As the name reflects, it is a technique in which the ailments are treated by applying pressure on specific acu points spread throughout the body. These points are located on imaginary lines called meridians.

These meridians are:
- Lung Meridian
- Large Intestine Meridian
- Stomach Meridian
- Spleen Meridian
- Heart Meridian
- Small Intestine Meridian
- Bladder Meridian
- Kidney Meridian
- Pericardium Meridian

- Triple Warmer Meridian
- Gall Bladder Meridian
- Liver Meridian
- Conception Vessel Meridian
- Governing Vessel Meridian

According to the TCM theory, this technique works by stimulating the meridian system to bring about relief by rebalancing yin, yang and chi (also called "qi").

Chi can not be exactly defined but in a way we may call it life force. In Japan it is called *Qi* or *Ki*; In India and Hinduism it is *Prana*; in Arabian countries and Islam it is *Barraka*; in Hebrew it is *Rauch*; Polynesians call it *Mana*.

Bony Landmarks:

The bony landmarks are important in term of finding and identifing the acu points.

Cranium:
The main landmarks on the cranium are:

• *Cheekbone and arch (maxillary bone, zygomatic bone, and zygomatic arch):* It runs from the ear to the nose. Firstly start with placing your fingers in front of your ear to palpate the *zygomatic arch* (a part of the temporal bone). Now go tho the downward direction, then you'll feel the *zygomatic bone*. Now curve back up toward your nose to feel the *maxillary bone*.

• *Orbit of the eye (Eye socket):* To palpate the full orbit, place your fingers on your eyebrows where you can feel the upper border of the orbit. Now run your fingers all along this bony circle.

• *Occipital protuberance:* Put your fingers behind your head and feel the hollow on the junction of the end of skull and the spinal column. Palpate the bony protuberances on either side of the hollow. It is the *Occipital protuberance.*

Shoulder Blades and Vertebrae:
The main landmarks on the shoulder blade and vertebrae are:

• *Vertebrae:* There are 7 vertebrae in the neck (cervical), 12 vertebrae in the midback where the ribs attached behind (thoracic), and 5 vertebrae in the low back (lumbar).

• *Shoulder Blade (scapula):* The two shoulder blades are placed on each side of your spinal column. These are triangular in shape. We need to palpate 4 main landmarks.

o *Inner border:* It is the edge of the blade closest to the spinal column.
o *Outer border:* It is the outer edge of the shoulder blade.
o *Superior angle:* Follow the inner border upwards and once you reach the sharp point on top of the border.
o *Inferior angle:* This is the lowermost point of the shoulder blade.

Chest and Shoulder:
The main landmarks on the chest are:

• *Chest bone (sternum):* It is in the bone in the middle of your chest. It has three parts: the upper part which connects with the collarbones (clavicle) is called the *Manubrium*, the middle part is called the *Body*, and the lower little part is called the *zyphoid process.*

• *Collar Bones (clavicals):* These are the horizontal bones connecting the upper part of the chest bone and the point of the shoulder.

• *Point of the shoulder (acromium processes):* This is the point where the collar bones meet the shoulder blades. It can be felt at the top of the shoulder.

Arm and Hand:
The main landmarks on the arm and hand are:

• *Deltoid tuberosity:* It is a bump located on the outside of the upper part of arm bone (where the doctors give injection).

• *Elbow bone (olecranon process):* Bend your elbow and the point of bone you find on the back of elbow is the *olecranon process*.

• *Lateral epicondyle:* Bend your elbow and the point of bony elevation you find on the outer side of the elbow is the *Lateral epicondyle.*
• *Medical epicondyle:* Bend your elbow and the point of bony elevation you find on the inner side of the elbow is the *Medial epicondyle.*

• *Wrist bone (ulnar tuberosity):* You can find it as a bony elevation on the little fingure's side of the back of your wrist.
• *Metacarpals:* These are the five bones that go from the wrist bones to the fingers — just like the metatarsals go from the anklebones to the toes. Feel the areas between the bones where the tendons run. These areas are important for point location.

Hip, pelvic, and buttock bones:
The main landmarks on the Hip, pelvic, and buttock bones are:

• *Hipbone Point (ASIS):* It can be found on either side of the lower stomach.

• *Top of the hipbone (iliac crest):* Move your fingers upward and backward starting from the Hipbone Point (ASIS). The bony border you feel all the way is the *Top of the hipbone (iliac crest).*

• *Pubic bone:* It can be felt between the two Hipbone Point (ASIS).

• *Sacrum:* It is a triangular bone with the vertex downwards at the bottom of your spinal column.

Knee bones and joints:
The main landmarks on the Hip, pelvic, and buttock bones are:

• *Kneecap (patella):* Straighten your leg and place your hand over the upper part of the knee. You can feel a small movable bone. It is the *Kneecap (patella).*

• *Knee bump (tibial tuberosity):* The first bony elevation below the Kneecap (patella) and on the uppermost part of the shinbone is *Knee bump (tibial tuberosity).*

• *Outer side of knee (fibular head):* It can be palpated as a bony elevation on the outer side of the knee joint at almost the same level as the *Knee bump (tibial tuberosity).*

Ankle and Foot:
The main landmarks on the ankle and foot are:

• *The outer anklebone (lateral malleolus):* You can palpate it as a big bony prominance on the outer side of your ankle. It is a part of the fibula bone.

• *Outer leg bone (fibula):* You can palpate it by moving your hand upward from the *outer anklebone (lateral malleolus)* to the knee.

• *Inner anklebone (medial malleolus):* It is situated on the inner side of the ankle just like the *outer anklebone (lateral malleolus)* but on its opposite side.

• *Shinbone (tibia):* It can be palpated on the front of the leg (shin).

Meridians:

The meridian is a hypothetical path which is believed to circulate *chi* flows through it.

There are 20 meridians which include 12 *Regular Meridians* and 8 *Extraordinary Meridians.* The 12 Regular Meridians are named by the organs they govern. Six of the Regular Meridians start or stop in the hands, and other six of them start or stop in the feet.

Cun:

It is the standard unit of measurement for the body used in acupuncture. It is required to locate the acu points and measure the distance from point.

One cun: It is equal to the width of the thumb, in the middle, at the crease.

One and Half Cun: It is equal to the combined breadth of two fingers (index and middle).

Three cun: It is equal to the combined breadth of the four fingers (except the thumb).

Twelve cun: It is equal to the distance from the elbow crease to the wrist crease.

Pressure Application:

The point should be pressed by finger or some blunt object.

If you get the point correctly, it will feel somewhat different on pressing. You may feel the point sore, tense or aching etc., but it confirms that you are pressing a acu point.

There is no hard and fast rule regarding the amount of pressure, but as per the general guideline, the pressure should be firm enough so that it "hurts good".

There is no hard and fast rule regarding the duration of the pressure applied on the points. But it may range from less than half a second to two minutes.

Warning:

Do not apply pressure in the following conditions.
- Bleeding
- Bruises
- Contagious Diseases
- Contusions
- Deep emotional trauma
- Fractures
- Infections
- Inflammation (signs of Redness + Swelling + Heat + Dysfunction)
- Prolapsed Intervertebral Disc (PIVD)

- Severe spinal trauma
- Severe swelling (edema)
- Sprains
- Strains
- Surgery
- Varicose Veins

3 GENERAL POINTS FOR TICS

During my practice I have found the following points very effective. These points may be used in all types of the tics:

1. GV20
2. LI4
3. P6
4. HT7
5. ST36
6. GB34

GV20:
Location: It is situated midway on a line connecting the apex of both ears, 5 cun above midpoint of anterior hairline, and 7 cun above the midpoint of the posterior hairline.

LI4:
Location: It is situated between the 1st and 2nd metacarpal bones on the back side (dorsum) of the hand.

P6:
Location: It is situated 2 cun above the the middle point (P7)

of the transverse crease of the wrist between palmaris longus and flexor carpi radialis tendons.

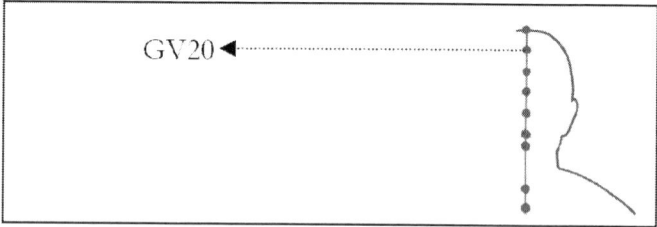

GV20

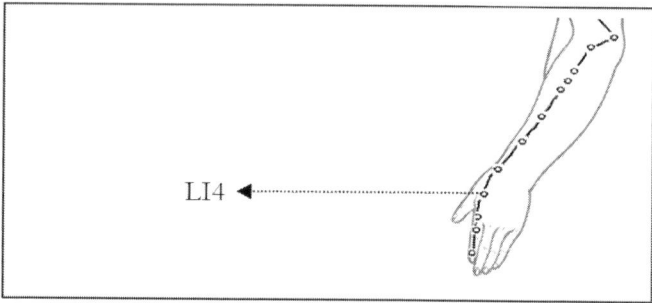

LI4

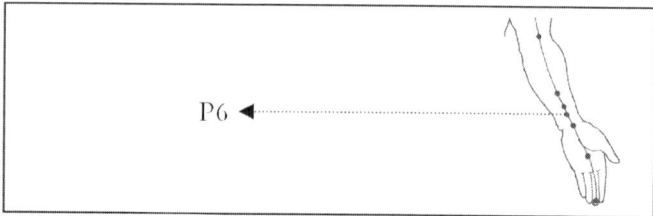

P6

HT7:

Location: It is situated in the small depression between the pisiform and ulna bones, on the anteromedial side of the transverse crease of the wrist with the palm facing up.

ST36:

Location: It is situated 3 cun below ST35 slightly lateral to the anterior crest of the tibia.

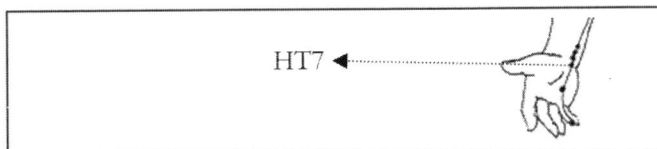

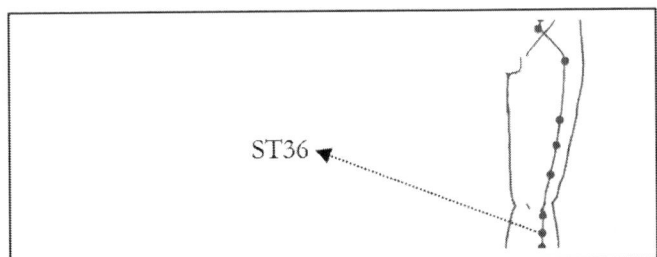

GB34:

Location: It is situated in a depression anterior and inferior to the head of the fibula.

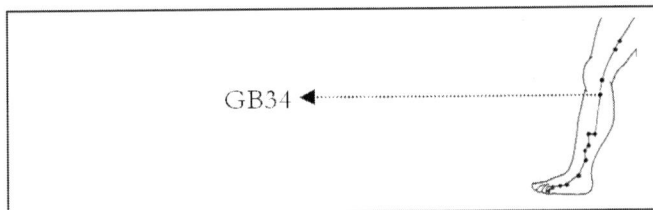

4 TICS OF THE EYE

During my practice I have found the following points very effective in the tics of the eye.

1. GV20
2. ST8
3. GB14
4. GB20
5. GB34
6. LI4
7. HT7
8. LV2
9. BL58

GV20:

Location: It is situated midway on a line connecting the apex of both ears, 5 cun above midpoint of anterior hairline, and 7 cun above the midpoint of the posterior hairline.

ST8:

Location: It is situated at the corner of the forehead.

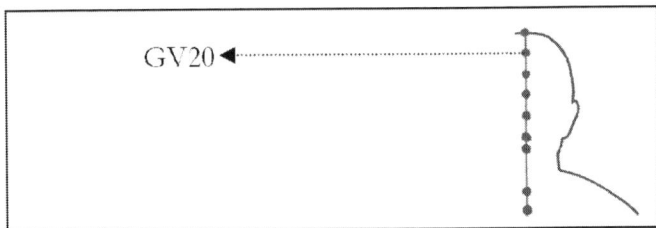

GV20

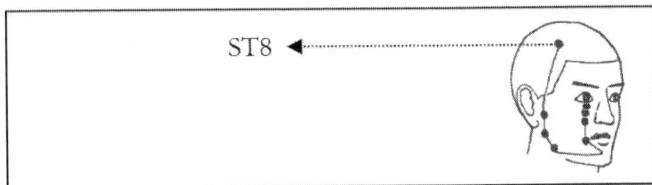

ST8

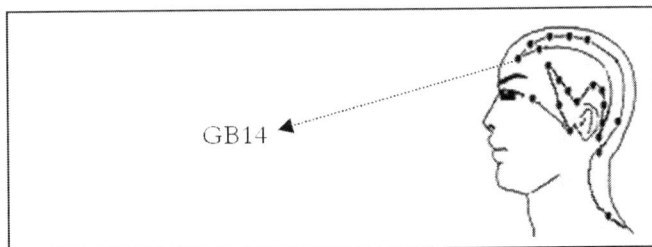

GB14

GB14:

Location: It is situated on the forehead 1 cun above the midpoint of the eyebrow, straight above the pupil.

GB20:

Location: It is situated in the depression created between the origins of the Sternocleidomastoid and Trapezius muscles, at the junction of the occipital and nuchal regions, lateral to the body midline.

GB34:

Location: It is situated in a depression anterior and inferior to the head of the fibula.

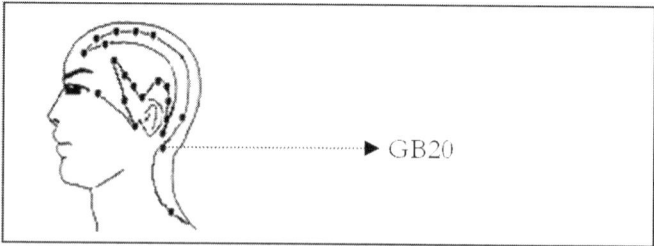

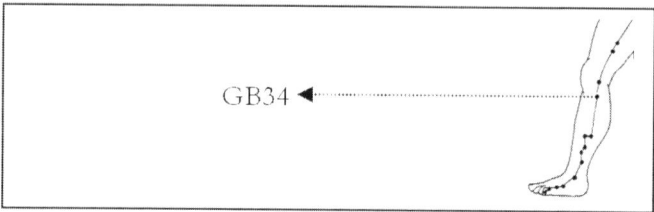

LI4:

Location: It is situated between the 1st and 2nd metacarpal bones on the back side (dorsum) of the hand.

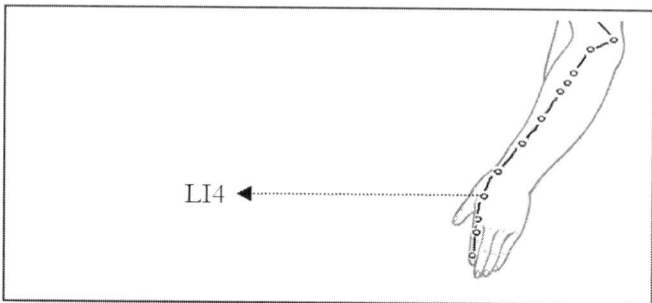

HT7:

Location: It is situated in the small depression between the pisiform and ulna bones, on the anteromedial side of the transverse crease of the wrist with the palm facing up.

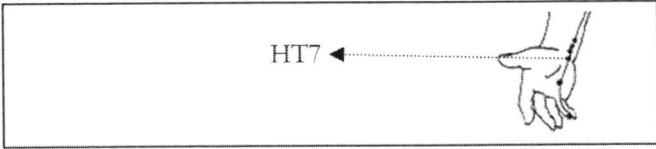

LV2:

Location: It is situated proximal to the margin of the web on dorsum of the foot between the 1st and 2nd toes.

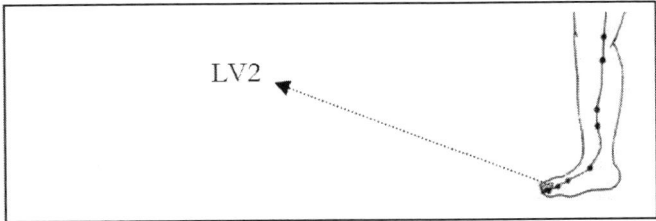

BL58:

Location: It is situated on the posterior border of the fibula, 7 cun above BL60, approx 1 cun lateral and inferior to BL57.

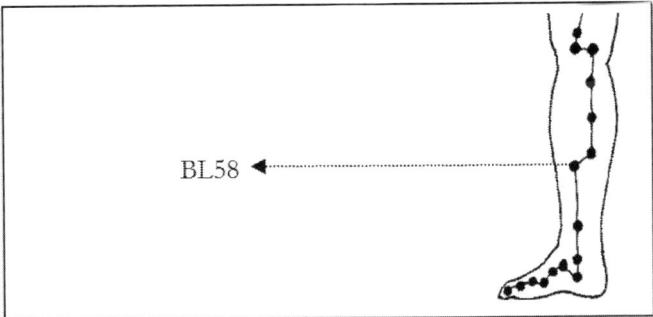

5 TICS OF THE FACE

During my practice I have found the following points very effective in the tics of the face.

1. TW17
2. GV20
3. ST4
4. ST36
5. SI18
6. SI19
7. LI4
8. HT7
9. P6
10. GB34

TW17:
Location: It is situated in a depression between the mandible and the mastoid process posterior to the lobule of the ear.

GV20:
Location: It is situated midway on a line connecting the apex of both ears, 5 cun above midpoint of anterior hairline, and

7 cun above the midpoint of the posterior hairline.

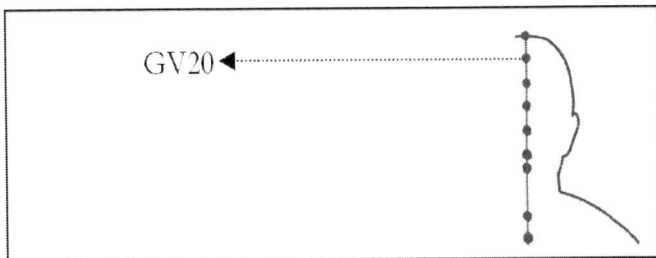

ST4:

Location: It is situated outer to the corner of the mouth, straight below the pupil.

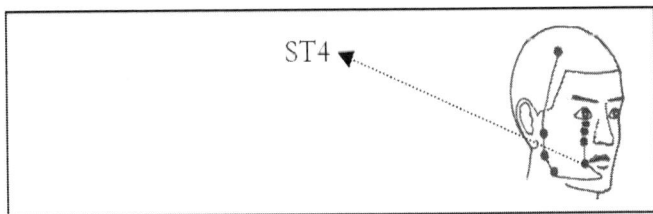

ST36:

Location: It is situated 3 cun below ST35 slightly lateral to the anterior crest of the tibia.

SI18:

Location: It is situated in a depression on the lower border of the zygomatic bone, straight below the outer canthus of the eye.

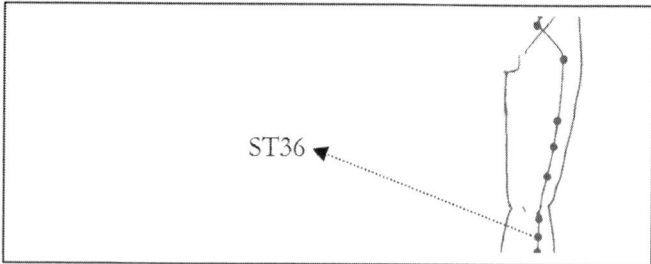

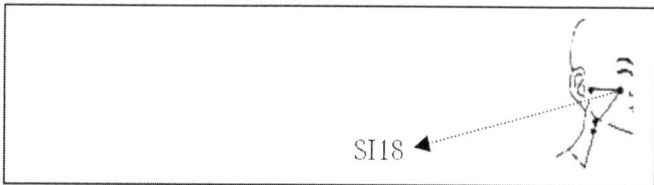

SI19:

Location: It is situated in a depression formed when mouth is opened, posterior to the condyloid process of the mandible.

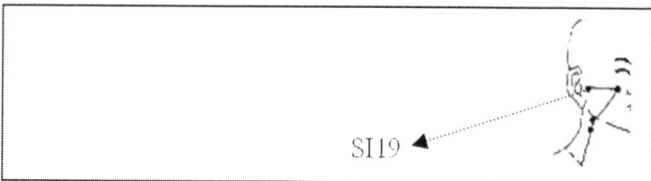

LI4:

Location: It is situated between the 1st and 2nd metacarpal bones on the back side (dorsum) of the hand.

HT7:

Location: It is situated in the small depression between the pisiform and ulna bones, on the anteromedial side of the transverse crease of the wrist with the palm facing up.

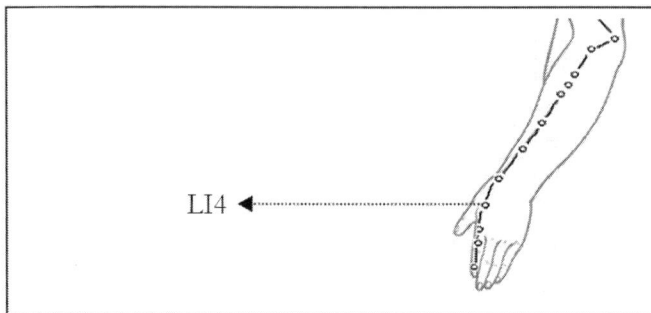

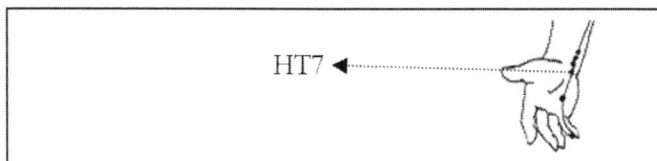

P6:

Location: It is situated 2 cun above the the the middle point (P7) of the transverse crease of the wrist between palmaris longus and flexor carpi radialis tendons.

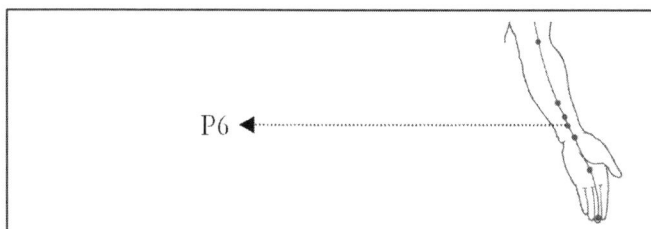

GB34:

Location: It is situated in a depression anterior and inferior to the head of the fibula.

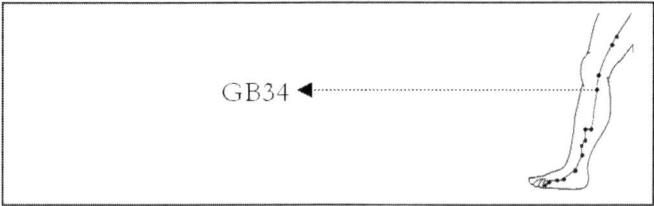

GB34

5 TICS OF THE NECK

During my practice I have found the following points very effective in the tics of the neck.

1. GB20
2. GB21
3. GB34
4. GV20
5. BL11
6. BL62
7. HT7
8. P6
9. LU7
10. ST36

GB20:

Location: It is situated in the depression created between the origins of the Sternocleidomastoid and Trapezius muscles, at the junction of the occipital and nuchal regions, lateral to the body midline.

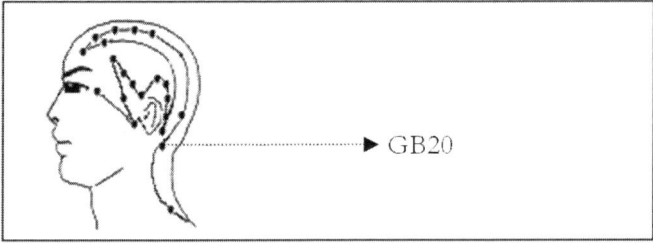

GB21:

Location: It is situated at the highest point of the trapezius muscle, midway between the spinous process of C7 and the acromion process.

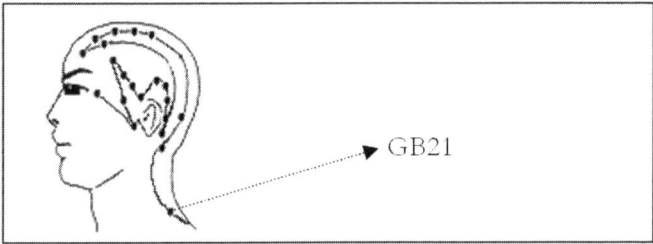

GB34:

Location: It is situated in a depression anterior and inferior to the head of the fibula.

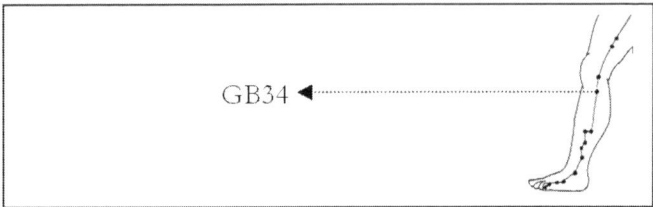

GV20:

Location: It is situated midway on a line connecting the apex of both ears, 5 cun above midpoint of anterior hairline, and 7 cun above the midpoint of the posterior hairline.

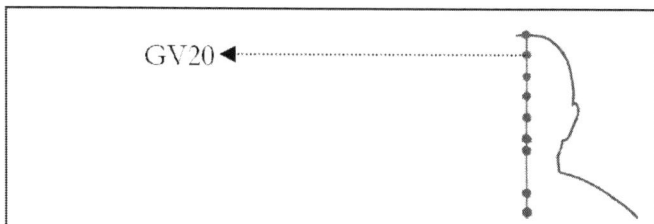

BL11:

Location: It is situated 1.5 cun lateral to the body midline at the level of the spinous process of T1. (from the midline to the medial border of the scapula is considered 3 cun)

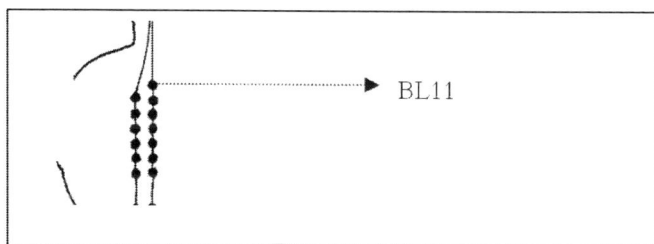

BL62:

Location: It is situated in a depression below the lateral malleolus.

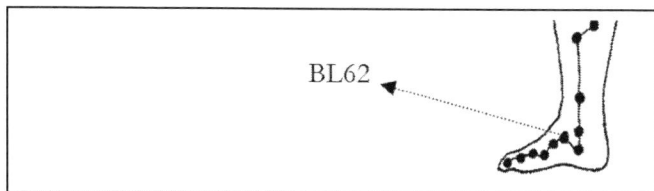

HT7:

Location: It is situated in the small depression between the pisiform and ulna bones, on the anteromedial side of the transverse crease of the wrist with the palm facing up.

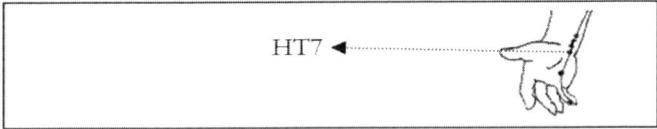

P6:

Location: It is situated 2 cun above the the middle point (P7) of the transverse crease of the wrist between palmaris longus and flexor carpi radialis tendons.

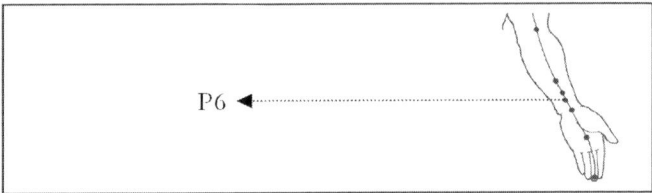

LU7:

Location: It is situated 1.5 cun above the transverse crease of the wrist, superior to the bony elevation in the wrist on thethumb side (styloid process of the radius).

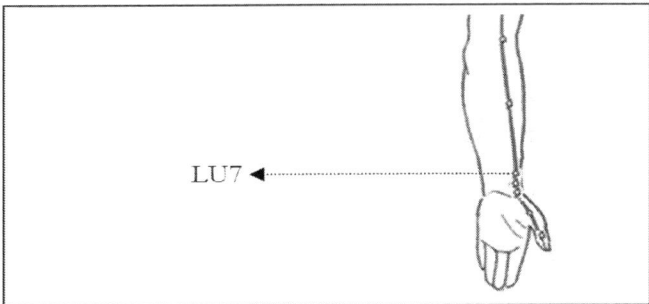

ST36:

Location: It is situated 3 cun below ST35 slightly lateral to the anterior crest of the tibia.

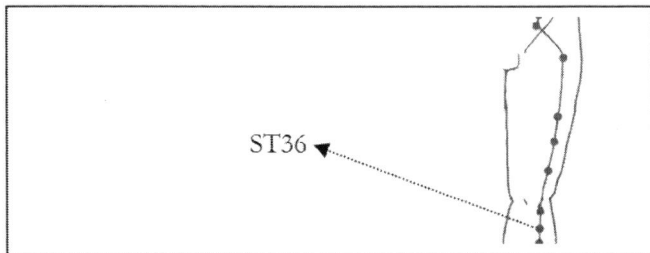

APPENDIX

———

CHARTS OF THE MEREDIANS

DR. KRISHNA N. SHARMA

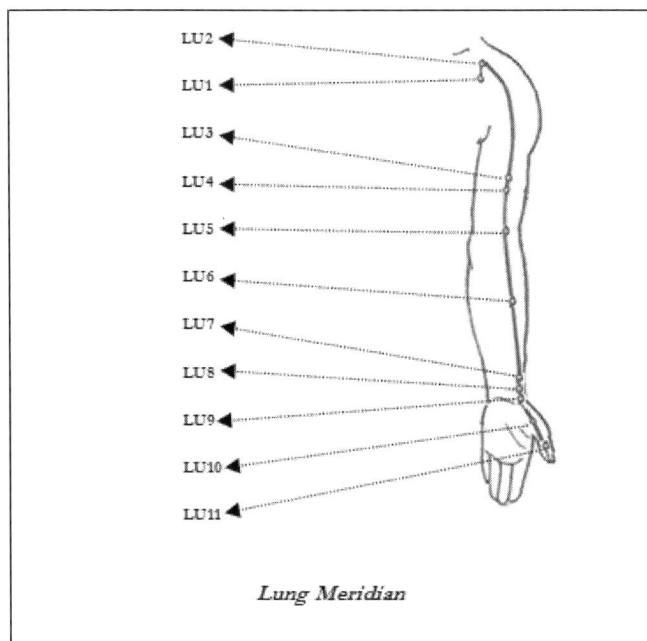

LU2
LU1
LU3
LU4
LU5
LU6
LU7
LU8
LU9
LU10
LU11

Lung Meridian

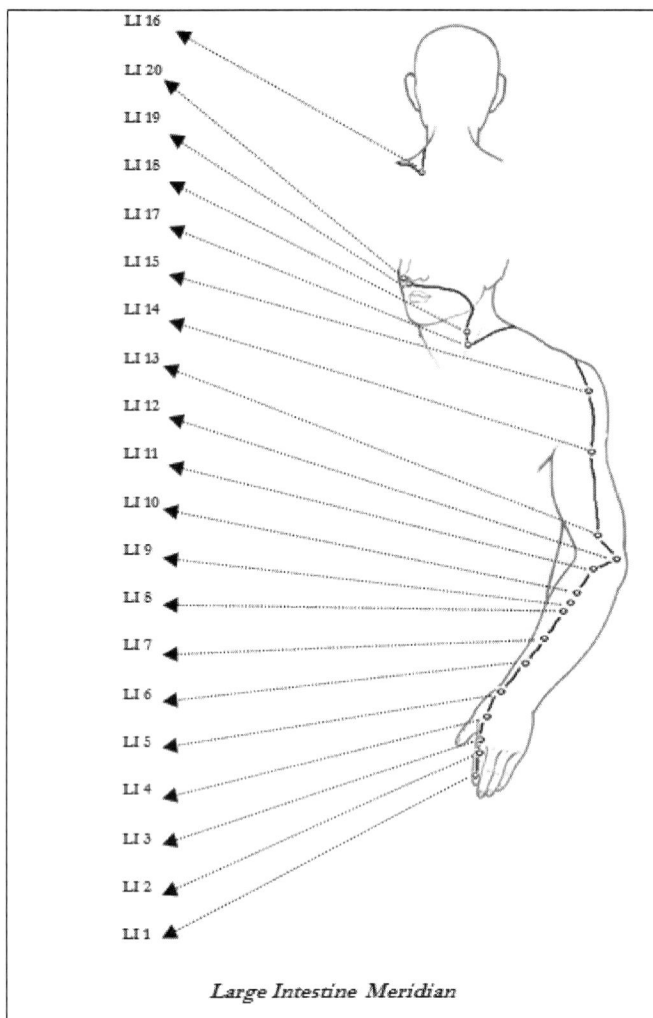

LI 16
LI 20
LI 19
LI 18
LI 17
LI 15
LI 14
LI 13
LI 12
LI 11
LI 10
LI 9
LI 8
LI 7
LI 6
LI 5
LI 4
LI 3
LI 2
LI 1

Large Intestine Meridian

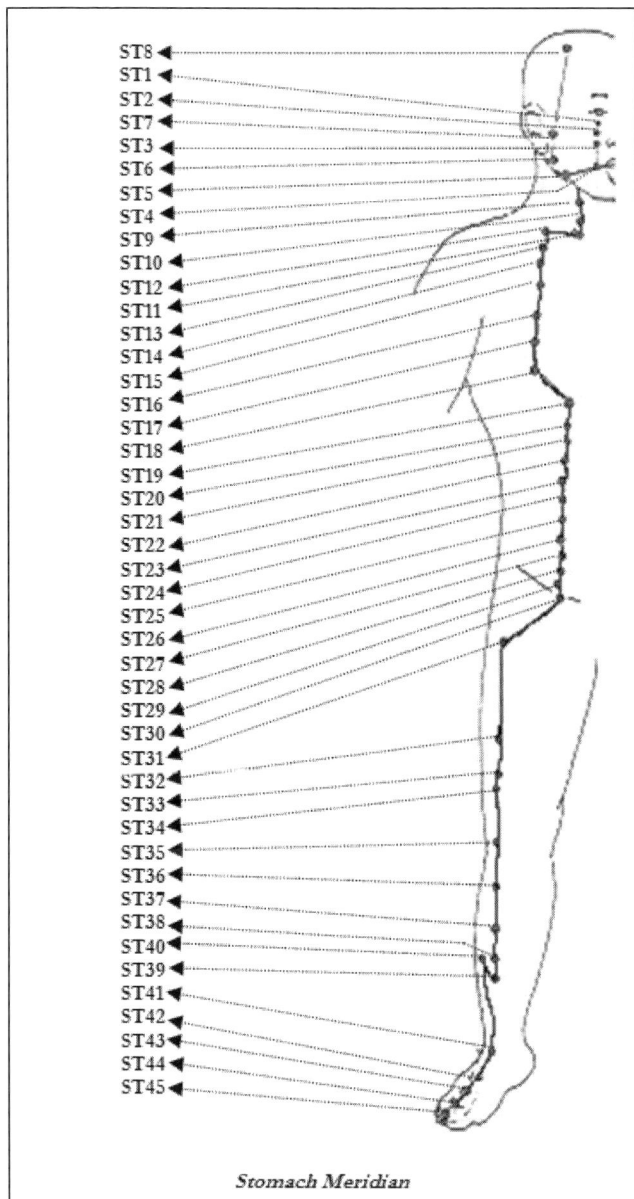

ST8
ST1
ST2
ST7
ST3
ST6
ST5
ST4
ST9
ST10
ST12
ST11
ST13
ST14
ST15
ST16
ST17
ST18
ST19
ST20
ST21
ST22
ST23
ST24
ST25
ST26
ST27
ST28
ST29
ST30
ST31
ST32
ST33
ST34
ST35
ST36
ST37
ST38
ST40
ST39
ST41
ST42
ST43
ST44
ST45

Stomach Meridian

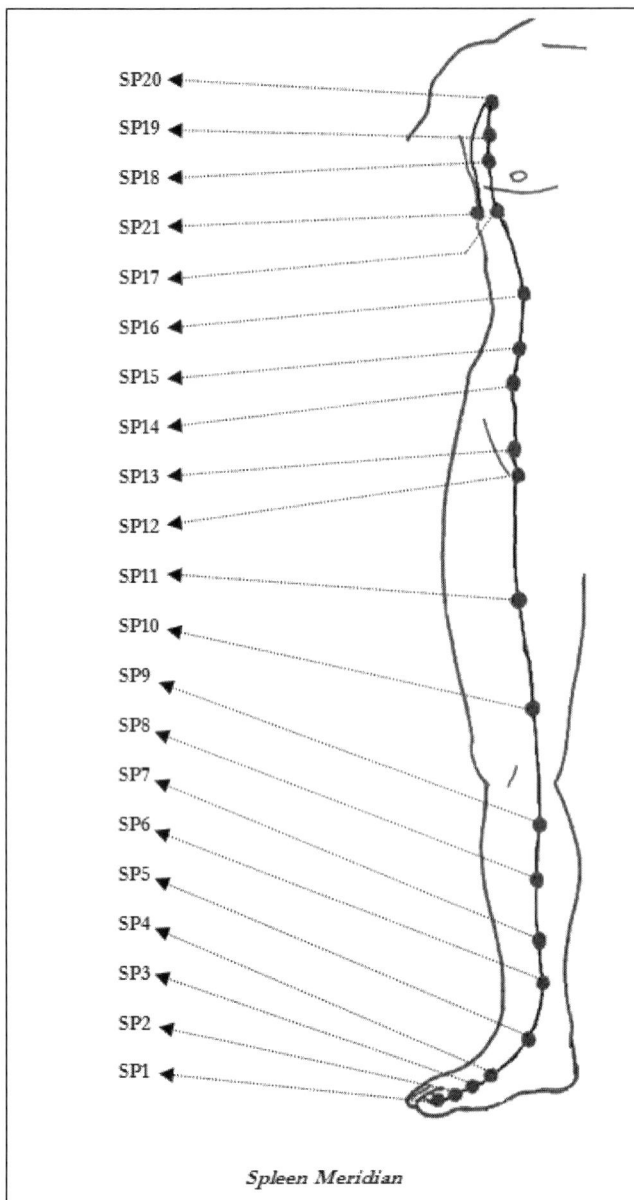

SP20
SP19
SP18
SP21
SP17
SP16
SP15
SP14
SP13
SP12
SP11
SP10
SP9
SP8
SP7
SP6
SP5
SP4
SP3
SP2
SP1

Spleen Meridian

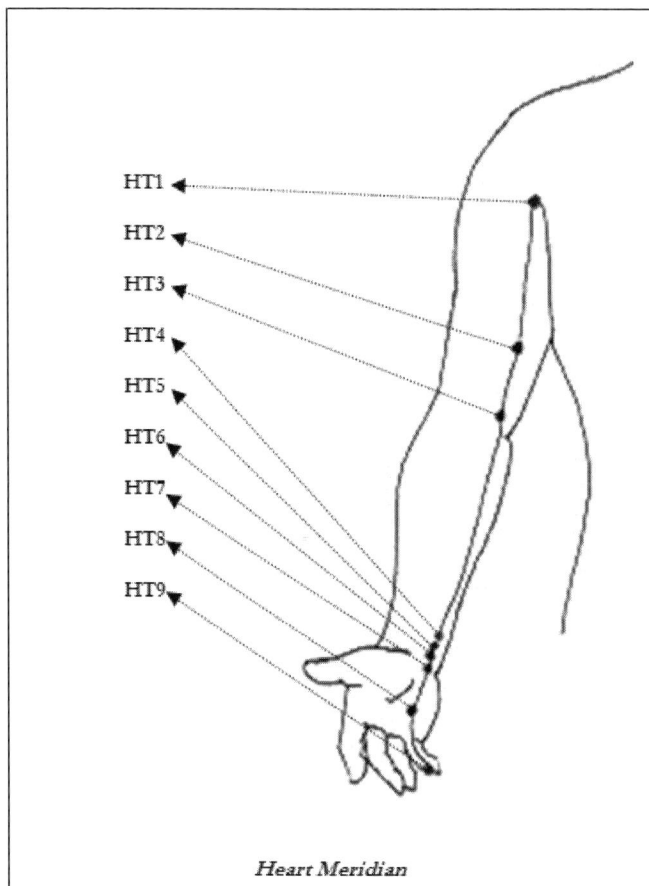

Heart Meridian

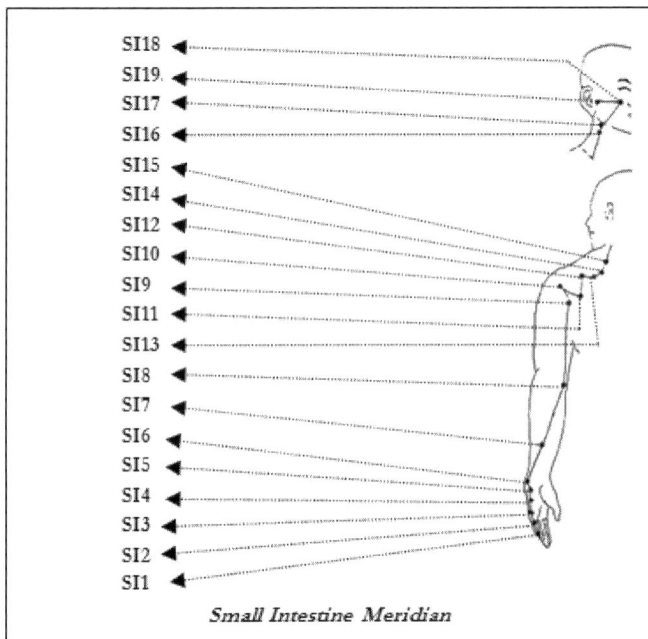

SI18
SI19
SI17
SI16
SI15
SI14
SI12
SI10
SI9
SI11
SI13
SI8
SI7
SI6
SI5
SI4
SI3
SI2
SI1

Small Intestine Meridian

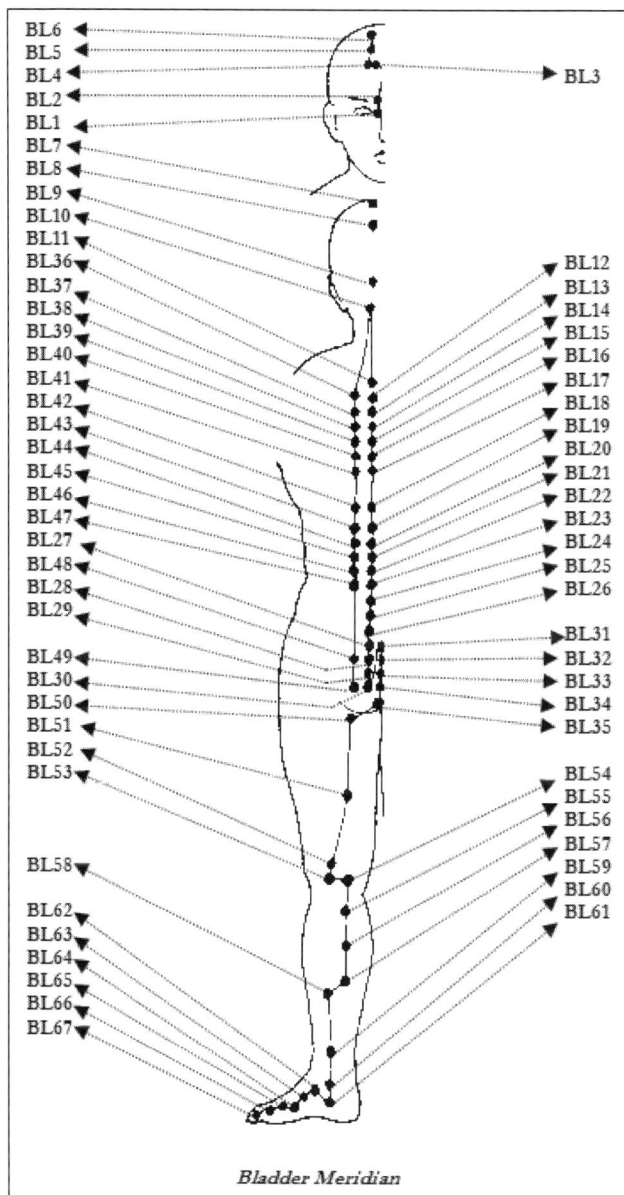

BL6
BL5
BL4
BL2
BL1
BL7
BL8
BL9
BL10
BL11
BL36
BL37
BL38
BL39
BL40
BL41
BL42
BL43
BL44
BL45
BL46
BL47
BL27
BL48
BL28
BL29
BL49
BL30
BL50
BL51
BL52
BL53
BL58
BL62
BL63
BL64
BL65
BL66
BL67

BL3
BL12
BL13
BL14
BL15
BL16
BL17
BL18
BL19
BL20
BL21
BL22
BL23
BL24
BL25
BL26
BL31
BL32
BL33
BL34
BL35
BL54
BL55
BL56
BL57
BL59
BL60
BL61

Bladder Meridian

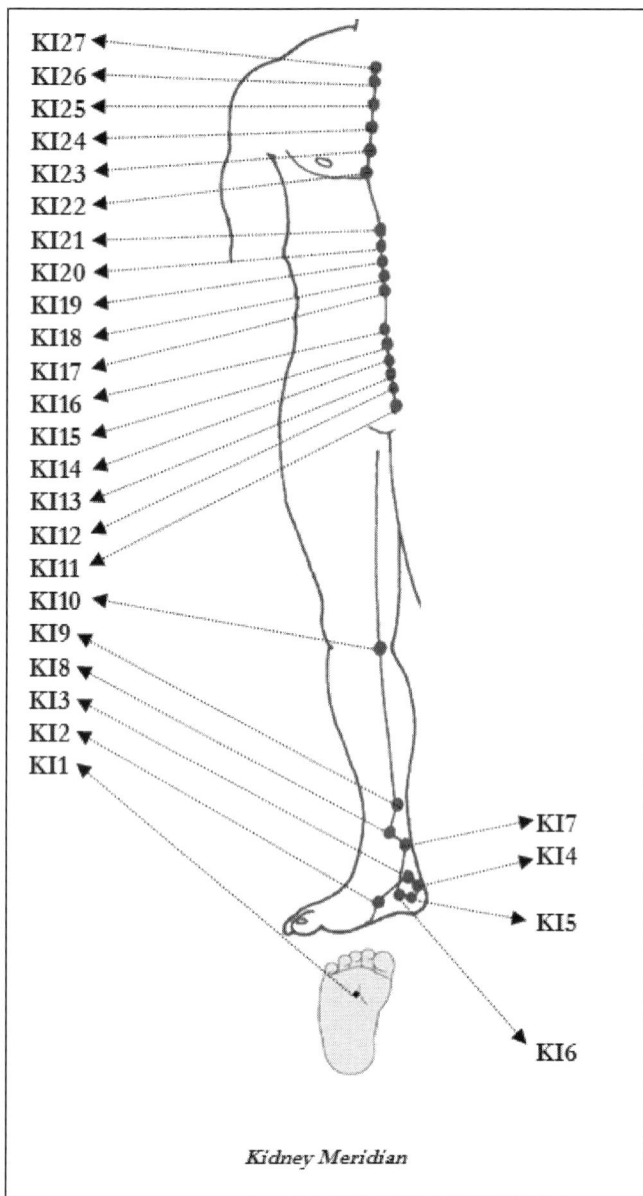

Kidney Meridian

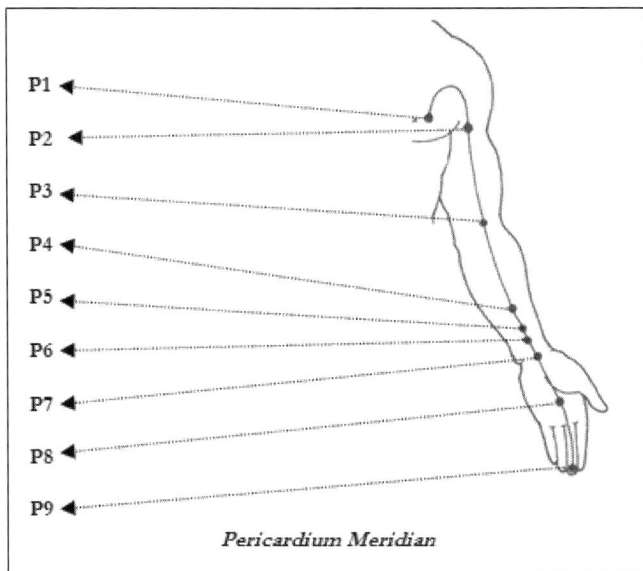

P1
P2
P3
P4
P5
P6
P7
P8
P9

Pericardium Meridian

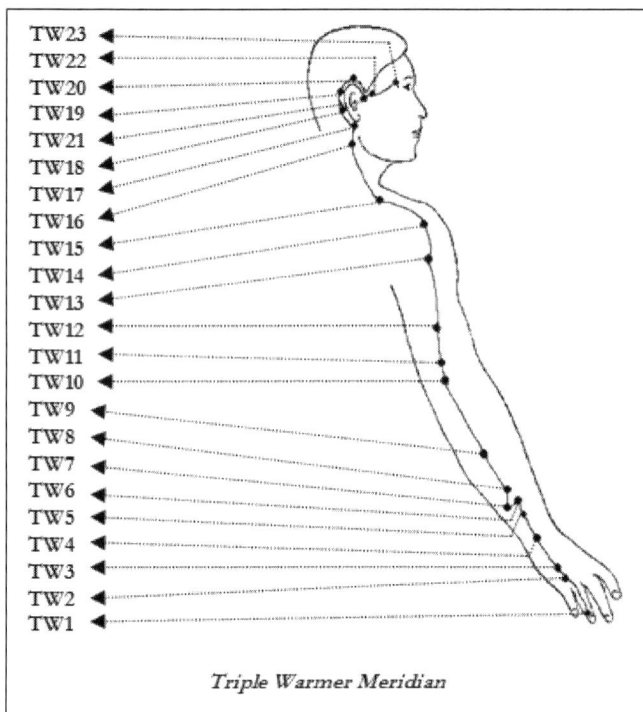

TW23
TW22
TW20
TW19
TW21
TW18
TW17
TW16
TW15
TW14
TW13
TW12
TW11
TW10
TW9
TW8
TW7
TW6
TW5
TW4
TW3
TW2
TW1

Triple Warmer Meridian

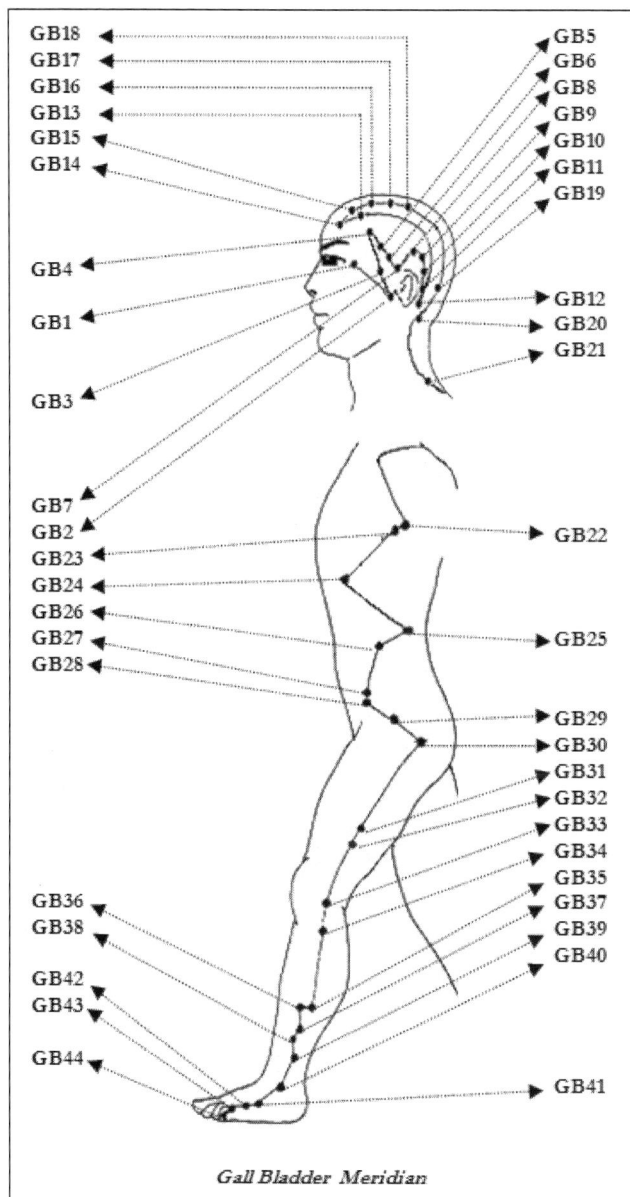

GB18
GB17
GB16
GB13
GB15
GB14

GB4

GB1

GB3

GB7
GB2
GB23
GB24
GB26
GB27
GB28

GB36
GB38

GB42
GB43

GB44

GB5
GB6
GB8
GB9
GB10
GB11
GB19

GB12
GB20
GB21

GB22

GB25

GB29
GB30
GB31
GB32
GB33
GB34
GB35
GB37
GB39
GB40

GB41

Gall Bladder Meridian

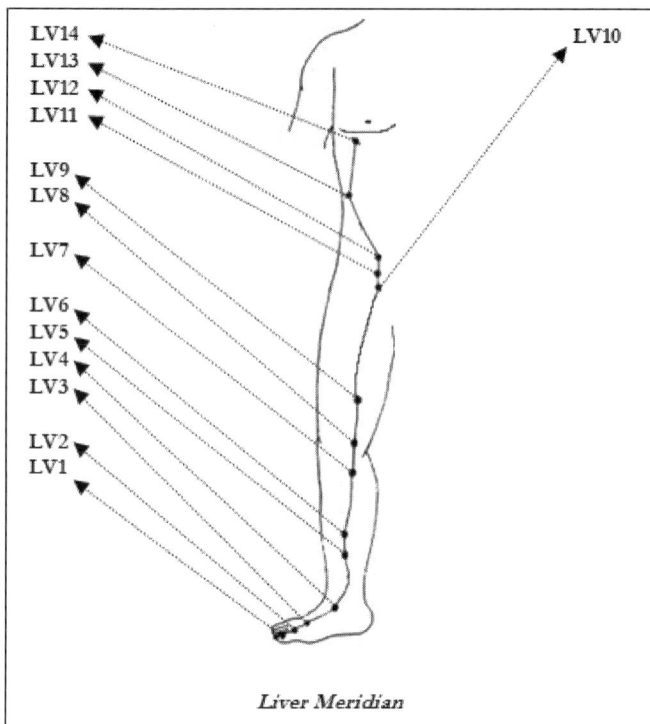

Liver Meridian

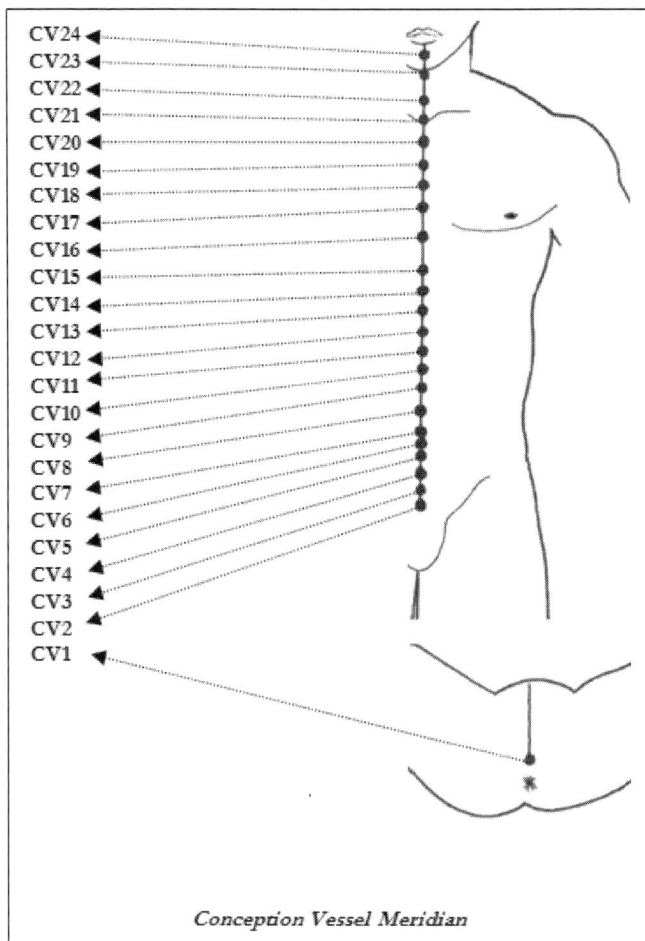

CV24
CV23
CV22
CV21
CV20
CV19
CV18
CV17
CV16
CV15
CV14
CV13
CV12
CV11
CV10
CV9
CV8
CV7
CV6
CV5
CV4
CV3
CV2
CV1

Conception Vessel Meridian

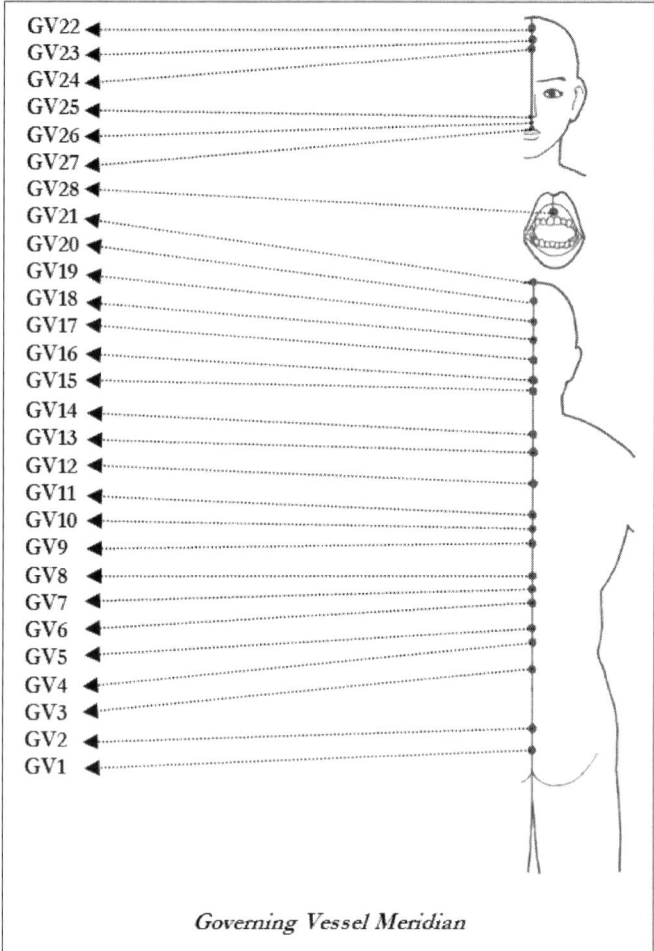

Governing Vessel Meridian

ABOUT THE AUTHOR

Dr. Krishna N. Sharma born in Muhammadabad Gohana, District Mau, U.P., India on December 24th is an Author, Medical Professional and Educator. He is founder Editor of the Scientific Research Journal of India and founder Gen. Secretary of the Online Physio Community, India. He writes health articles and columns in various newspapers and magazines of India and Bangladesh. So far he has written and edited 34 books and has made 2 world records.

AUTHOR CONTACT

Dr. L. Sharma Campus, Muhammadabad Gohna, Mau, U.P. 276403, India
Ph: +91-9320699167, 9305835734
Email: dr.krisharma@gmail.com
Web: http://www.krishna.info.ms

DR. KRISHNA N. SHARMA

6323450R00032

Made in the USA
San Bernardino, CA
05 December 2013